I Want To LIVE!

By
Patricia A. Fisher

Published by
ITSMEEE™ Industries
Aurora, CO
USA

Patricia A. Fisher

I Want To LIVE!
Copyright © 2004 by Patricia A. Fisher

Published by ITSMEEE™ Industries

All rights reserved, including the right to reproduce this book or portions thereof in any form. No part of this book covered by the copyrights hereon may be reproduced or copied in any form or by any means – graphic, electronic, or mechanical, including but not limited to, photocopying, recording, taping, scanning, or information storage and retrieval systems – without the express written permission of the author, Patricia A. Fisher.

All interior art by Patricia A. Fisher
Book layout and design by Patricia A. Fisher
Book production and technical advice by D. H. Fisher
Cover production and design by
NZ Graphics, Lakewood, CO

Printed in the United States of America

First Edition

Library of Congress Control Number: 2004095613
Old ISBN: 0-9677231-5-9
New ISBN: 978-0-9677231-5-0

Other Titles by Patricia A. Fisher

With Love ITSMEEE™
Copyright © 1997 by Patricia A. Fisher

With Love ITSMEEE™ II
Copyright © 1998 by Patricia A. Fisher

Introducing Number III, ITSMEEE™
Copyright © 1999 by Patricia A. Fisher

ITSMEEE™ On My Journey Home
Copyright © 1999 by Patricia A. Fisher
ITSMEEE™ Industries

Hello, ITSMEEE™ Again
Copyright © 2002 by Patricia A. Fisher
ITSMEEE™ Industries

ITSMEEE™ Beneath the Grey
An Autobiography
Copyright © 2003 by Patricia A. Fisher
ITSMEEE™ Industries

Other Titles (Continued) By Patricia A. Fisher

From This Day Forward
Copyright © 2003 by Patricia A. Fisher
ITSMEEE™ Industries

I Want to LIVE!
Copyright © 2004 by Patricia A. Fisher
ITSMEEE™ Industries

Walk a Mile in Our Shoes
Copyright © 2005 by Patricia A. Fisher
ITSMEEE™ Industries

The Favor I Owe the World
Copyright © 2005 by Patricia A. Fisher
ITSMEEE™ Industries

Home Is Where We Park It!
Copyright © 2008 by Pat Fisher
Funhous Publishing

The Absence of Awful
Copyright © 2012 by Patricia A. Fisher
ITSMEEE™ Industries

Roses are red.
Violets are blue.
Straight from my heart,
I love you…

Roses are red.
Violets are blue.
Straight from my heart,
I love me, too…

Table of Contents:

I Want To Live 1
I Walk in Gratitude 11
Eternity 15
Dennis' Aim 21
Hello, Sweet Friend 25
Beginner's Luck 31
A Ray of Hope 35
Only Human 39
Never Say Hi 43
Dear Mr. Henneman (A) 51
Dear Mr. Henneman (B) 57
Dear Mr. Henneman (C) 65
Dear Mr. Henneman (D) 69
Dear Mr. Henneman (E) 75
Chains 83
Out of My Control 87
Laugh at the Devil 99
Buried Alive 103
My Sisters, With Love 109
My Dennis 113

Table of Contents Continued:

Travel section:

Been There........................ 123
Winding River 143
Moab or Bust 153
Sages and Grey 161
Out On the Prairie 167
Colorado, I'm Home............ 186

Patricia A. Fisher

Dear reader most kind,

This is yet another book inspired by you and my higher power. Without that steady flow of words and ideas, I would not be an author. I could not send my love to all of you, because my love seems to come from a place of innocence and divinity.

I thank some kids from the Jesus Christ of Latter Day Saints. They came by our house and shared their wondrous story. They shared the way they talk to God, and I found myself doing it the same way.

The second time they came to our house, I said the prayer, and a warm presence washed over me.

I had no idea this was supposed to happen, and maybe the 'elders' didn't either. I just had this feeling that I was cleansed by a holy spirit, and that there was more room for the good stuff inside me.

I am not going off the deep end. It is the opposite. I have been more thankful, since these good spirits came to our home.

I am not trying to push you into any kind of belief. I just wanted to share my experience. I have been closer to my God ever since this happened.

I find myself saying thank you for things and people I already have in my life, and rarely ask for anything.

Patricia A. Fisher

It is like getting an answer to my prayer before I am finished praying...

I have difficulties just like anyone does, but now I talk to my higher power, even when I feel I'm in hell...

When I write, I have you in my thoughts, gentle reader. This way I am writing for all of us, and not just myself... I thank you for this. I thank you for giving me people to love and be with.

I Want to LIVE!

Again, I thank you for being a part of my journey.

Patricia A. Fisher

Patricia A. Fisher

I Want To Live

Dear heavenly Father,
I thank you for my life.
I thank you, though my burdens
Have laden me with strife.

There have been
Many times, God
When I have
Entertained

The thoughts
Of suicide, God
The times
My heart was pained.

Patricia A. Fisher

My mind still crashes
Way far down,
When things
Don't go my way.

A temper tantrum
Such as this
Causes me
To pay...

Yes, I said,
"A tantrum",
Like times
When I was young.

It came to me
Just lately.
To suicide,
I've clung.

I Want to LIVE!

Whenever
I get angry,
In a great
Big way,

I lose strength
In my body.
Into my bed
I lay.

I study all
The many ways
That I can
Kill myself.

I pray
And get no answers –
Though I don't
Ask for wealth.

Patricia A. Fisher

I ask for
Peace of mind.
I ask Him
To be near.

I ask that He
Return to me
My life
So full of cheer.

Without the
Intervention,
Of Dennis –
Oh so kind,

I might have
'Up and done it'
This plan
That's in my mind.

He speaks to me
So kindly –
That he loves
Me so.

Sometimes
Again, I'm angry.
He won't
Let me go…

So, now we're
In these mountains,
Giving me
New life.

I find that
It's worth living –
For I've less
Pain and strife.

I wake up.
The air is crisp,
And cool
As it can be.

I thank God
For everything
That He has
Given me...

This is when
He answers most –
When I am
Thanking Him,

For something
He's already done.
My life
Fills to the brim.

I Want to LIVE!

What is the use
Of being blessed,
When you don't know
'Twas done?

Count how many
Gifts you have,
And pray
For every one!

Dearest God,
I thank you
For giving life
To me,

And all the
Lovely toys I have.
Out here
My heart can see,

Patricia A. Fisher

Just what is
Important,
To live this life
Of mine.

It isn't buying
Diamond rings,
Although
They are divine!

It isn't all
The fancy clothes,
Although
They have their place.

I find that
What's important
Is being
Blessed with grace.

The gift of
Being able
To give
Or take in turn,

All the love
That comes your way
So you
No longer yearn,

Dear God,
My greatest gift,
Is nestled
Here inside.

It's that I've
Not succeeded,
When I could
Have died.

Patricia A. Fisher

So, here I am
Dear Father.
I give
What I can give.

I take this life
You've given me.
Dear God,
I want to live!

I Want to LIVE!

I Walk in Gratitude

If I were to write this piece in only a positive way, it would be like painting with just half of the colors. It would be sterile and only half the truth.

Those of you, who have read my books, know about a person going from one end of the continuum to the other. You, already, comprehend the wholeness of 'using all the colors', and you, have an idea, about most of what a human can experience.

I've told you of pain, struggle, hard times, and I've shared how one person answers these challenges.

I Want to LIVE!

Human lives are fraught with pain and discomfort, but we can also feel so much joy that we feel we might burst!

This is what I must share today. My heart is so full...

Just outside my window there is a family of robins. I sit and am in wonder of what is taking place. I chuckle from a part of myself that is innocent, and probably connected to my higher power.

Along toward night, a phenomenon takes place – a sunset... I call this time of day, 'Long Shadows'.

Patricia A. Fisher

As I watch in amazement, the world is transformed, and I am in awe of God's creativity.

I am struck by the inability to speak! This is usually when I pray in silence.

There are times when my heart, my mind, and my soul are in sync, and it is all I can do to keep my composure!

So I get up off my chair, and in appreciation for everything, I walk with sheer happiness that I am alive!

All my woes are gone for a while, and I smile.

This is when, without effort,
    I Walk in Gratitude...

Eternity

What would you do with a husband, who's perfect in almost every way? Could you measure up to him, when you're with him almost all the time?

Would you begin to feel less than him, or that you don't have his good sense? Maybe you were raised differently – on the wrong side of the tracks…

Then, one day, you find you have a gift that you do well. You find that you are worthwhile, because you have learned many things. You start to feel you're as good as anyone, and a part of everything! Life is simpler, and more fun.

All you had to do, to measure up, was be yourself, and respect the both of you. You took him down from that pedestal you had him on. Now he and you are more even.

You also disagree more, and each of you learn from the other. You confess to each other that you just want to be heard, but with both of you talking, you don't hear each other very well sometimes.

Now your hubby is only human, and he no longer has to be perfect. You no longer have to feel bad.

I Want to LIVE!

Patricia A. Fisher

Your husband and you will be
together for an eternity. You
didn't believe 'forever' would
ever happen to you! You love
him with all your heart, and
'forever' is just fine with you.
You hate it when you are apart...

So, when you speak
Of eternity,
You'd better know
What you said.

For dealing with words
Like eternity,
Start from
The day you wed.

The years come along,
And then go by –
One right after
The other...

All those years
Of being in love
Only with
Each other,

Say to you
There is a God,
And love
Is just a miracle!

Limited humans
Such as I
End up
Talking lyrical,

Telling how
You're even –
Each other
You adore.

Patricia A. Fisher

Two very equal
Partners,
In love
Forever more...

Dennis' Aim

You're my husband.
I'm your dame.
You need practice
With your aim!

When I go
To clean the 'pot',
On the floor,
I find a spot.

My dear man—
I will explain.
I surmise,
You have no aim!

Made you clean,
That little spot.
Then your aim
Improved a lot!

Patricia A. Fisher

If you let me

        Give you hugs,

You won't need

        So many drugs...

Patricia A. Fisher

Hello, Sweet Friend

Hello, sweet friend.
Are you having some fun?
What would happen,
If you were the one,

Who chuckled or laughed
At some little thing?
What would happen?
To make your heart sing!

Will it mean that you'll
Go out of control?
Or maybe your heart
Would jive with your soul.

What if your mind,
So stern and so strict,
Would let down its guard
With friends that you picked.

Where would you be,
Just laughing out loud,
All by yourself,
Or with a big crowd?

Is it something to fear –
That light airy mood?
Are you hugging the ground
Trying not to be rude?

Is it so strange
To feel good awhile?
Is it so odd,
If often you'd smile?

Are you afraid?
Are you hugging the ground?
Are you less of a target,
When life comes around?

I Want to LIVE!

What about you,
My sweet friend?
Is part of life
Passing you by?

Because those feelings
Are fearful,
How many tears
Do you cry?

Laughter's been known
To be healing,
Relaxing all of the stress.
It makes the road a lot easier.
This I do confess...

I know you lost your Mother.
Things have gotten you down.
Your girlfriend
Said goodbye to you.
So she's no longer around.

Patricia A. Fisher

Finances have become difficult.
You try so very hard!
People close to you
Don't understand.
No wonder you're on guard!

You have a lot to be proud of,
And you deserve respect.
You have responsibilities.
Yet I will be direct.

I promise not to leave you.
Forever, you're my friend.
If laughter's on your agenda,
We'll celebrate to the end.

You don't have to be a
Giggle box.
Just let yourself have joy.
If you get scared,
I'll hold your hand,
As if you were a boy.

I Want to LIVE!

Patricia A. Fisher

Gift yourself, my sweet friend.
Go out and have some fun!
Don't let your losses
Pull you down.
Don't let them make you run!

Don't hide inside
Your wonderful brain –
Though it has its place,
And walk a little bit taller,
With that handsome smile
On your face.

To my friend, Nemo.
With love,
From your friend, Pat.

Beginner's Luck

Dennis and I were camping up at Shadow Mountain Lake. On a rare occasion, we were joined by my sister, her hubby, and their two children, Tanya and Nick.

Some of us caught a fish. Some did not.

It was so exciting for the kids to be there! Nick proceeded to get campfire ashes all over him. At ten years of age, he was so cute, and happy to be covered with black soot. He was so entranced by the fire!

Tanya, age 13 or 14, was more interested in the challenges of fishing. She watched my progress and we talked for awhile.

Then she noticed a ten foot length of fishing line on the ground. It was complete, with a dried up worm on a hook. She picked it up and lowered it down the wall into the river.

After a couple of moments, she started squealing with delight! A good size trout was now on the other end of Tanya's line. This was enough to make her day, or maybe her whole year!

I Want to LIVE!

We then had enough fish for everyone. We cooked them on a small stove, in our ancient, little, hard-wall trailer.

Little Tanya's fish could have been 'beginner's luck', or maybe divine intervention, but it is yet another memory that leaves me smiling with my heart…

A Ray of Hope

It was as if I had gone to the bottom of the proverbial barrel, and then found a dime.

It shown like a ray of light, there within the darkness.

I was lifted up until I could see just over the rim of this barrel.

There I saw my whole family, glowing in this light... They had tears of love, and happiness, falling down their faces.

This was a day of reckoning and transformation. This was the day we reached out our hand to each other – a total absence of grief and bitterness.

Patricia A. Fisher

I thought, "My dears, this must be heaven!"

Then, I woke up in my own little bed, and sadly realized I was only dreaming...

Patricia A. Fisher

Only Human

Today was a clear and sunshiny day – a good day for taking a ride with someone you love.

I'm learning what it is to be only human, and to let others be the same.

We are all fallible, and at times a bit of a challenge to each other.

When we learn about our own hang-ups, not only those of others, we can actually begin to forgive through understanding.

I'm loving being out among people. There's an equality thing going on with me, and I feel a sense of belonging more than ever in my life.

When I pray, a lot of times I ask that all human beings feel they belong, and they are loved, at least once in their lives.

I use to take people's moods personally, but it isn't always about me! That person may be miles away in their thoughts, and need some space for a few moments. Now, I try to let them be...

I Want to LIVE!

I don't think people are living their uniqueness, if they don't have disagreements once in awhile.

A lot of times, differences can be celebrated, if they are handled with love, respect, and truth.

Maybe we should wear a sign:

"HANDLE WITH CARE. I'M ONLY HUMAN."

Never Say Hi

Never say hi
To a crow.
It might just
Answer back.

You may not ever
Get rid of it.
For these birds
Have a knack,

For overstaying
Their welcome.
They make just
Tons of noise!

They gather in trees
Above you.
Their conversation
Destroys,

Patricia A. Fisher

Any peace
And quiet
That you planned
For yourself.

For heaven sakes
Don't answer!
It's not good
For your health!

They keep you from
Your napping,
Or having
A nice meal,

Under the trees
Above you.
Perturbed is how
You'll feel!

I Want to LIVE!

Caw! Caw! Caw!
Is fun
When they
Begin.

One of the sounds
Of nature,
You'll hear it
Again and again.

At first you laugh
When it happens.
You offer up
Some food.

You find that you
Have friends for life.
For here's
The whole darn brood!

Patricia A. Fisher

That noise above you
Doubles.
Your hands go
Over your ears.

You then decide
To go away,
And have
A couple of beers.

You come back home
To your RV.
Guess what's happened
Now!

All those crows,
Your newest friends,
Are eating up
Your chow!

Isn't anything
Sacred?
Your hotdogs
Are now gone.

Your yummy marshmallows
Are no more.
You wait
Till crack of dawn.

You come outside
To find, again,
These crows
Are still around!

Instead of being
In the trees,
They're walking
On the ground,

Patricia A. Fisher

To find some
Tasty morsels
Your family
May have dropped.

You thought by now
Your feathered friends'
Invasion
Would've stopped!

That's what you get
For making friends
With loud
Obnoxious birds!

Never say hi
To a crow.
You may regret
Your words…

I Want to LIVE!

Patricia A. Fisher

Dear Mr. Henneman (A)

Dearest Mr. Henneman,
Why must I be so blue?

I try so very, very hard,
To do my work with you…

At times I feel
You'll give me up,

And no more
Therapy.

And just in time
You speak so kind—

(Good medicine
For me.)

Patricia A. Fisher

God bless you, Mr. Henneman.
There are no more like you.

For when you reach
Within your heart,

Your caring
Comes right through.

So thank you, Mr. Henneman.
Our work may not be done.

Even if it isn't,
At times we must have fun!

Just listen to a song bird,
Or smell a fresh cool rain,

Or take a trip
In the zoom-zoom car,

A smile
You will gain.

This will help you
Sleep at night,

And clear
Will be your brain.

This will help you
Help someone

Who might be
In some pain.

Patricia A. Fisher

Try looking
In your mirror.

I know that
You will see

A good and caring
Person,

Who's cared about
By me.

I choose to see your truth.
I also feel respect.

You seem to be a caring man.
'Tis easy to detect.

I Want to LIVE!

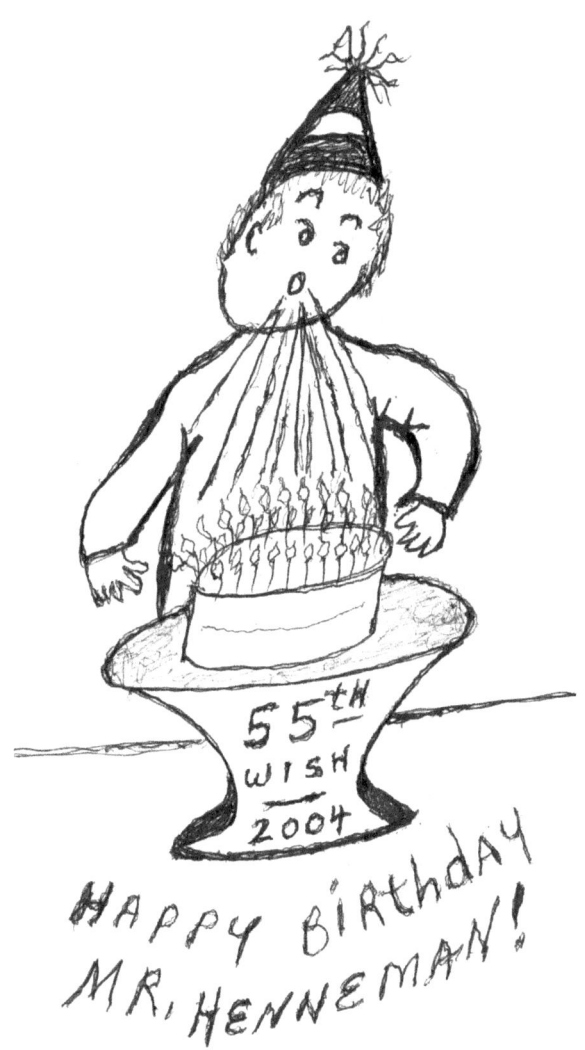

Patricia A. Fisher

For when I find I need a lot,
You don't run away.

You help me fight the demons,
And help me save the day.

You go above, and far beyond,
The duties that you're told.

This year you will be 55,
With wisdom good as gold.

Dear Mr. Henneman (B)

Dearest Mr. Henneman,
A big problem have I!
A happy day fell through,
And I just don't know why...

My friend and I enjoy
Being with each other.
He kind of moved into
The space of my sweet Mother.

I put him in her place.
For Mom was my good friend.
Since she passed away,
My heart just could not mend

I had three favorite people.
Miss Dee was one of these.
Mom was one, then Dennis.
Everything in threes.

Patricia A. Fisher

Then, all of a sudden,
Mom just passed away!
I was broken hearted.
I cried most everyday.

Miss Dee died one year later.
She just left this world!
I'd known her twenty years –
Back when my dreams unfurled.

My three most favorite people
Dwindled down to one.
My heart became real fearful.
I could not see the fun.

I use to spend those hours
Just talking on the phone,
To my beloved Mother—
More fond of her I've grown.

Patricia A. Fisher

Then, in a year or two
The pain still did not end.
I cry about my Mom.
She truly was my friend...

Dearest Mr. Henneman,
I need to ask of you,
Can my new friend, Nemo,
Make me feel less blue?

No romance between us,
'Cause I am married true,
Yet, just one marriage partner
Can't meet all needs for you.

So here we are with friendship,
My friend Nemo and me.
I brought him over to dinner.
My Dennis did agree.

Nemo is unusual—
A real good person, too.
Little by little we liked him,
And he liked us some, too.

He took me to his church.
I wasn't at my best.
Nemo seemed more quiet,
And I was put to test.

After church was over,
We didn't leave as planned.
Lunch was at the church.
My head was in the sand.

I was insecure,
When he asked of me,
"Do you want to stay?
We could eat for free."

Patricia A. Fisher

I just didn't answer,
Avoiding telling him,
I thought that we were going out
Just with me and him.

But I didn't say it—
What was on my mind.
I thought that his idea
Of going out was kind.

So, I ate mostly sugar—
On that cake or that pie.
I was not suppose to.
I eat too much, I die...

So, I felt somewhat angry,
At him, my newest friend.
I couldn't quite keep hidden
Some anger felt within.

So, Dearest Mr. Henneman,
I will tell you true…
Before I took my nap today,
I knew not what to do.

I've had a lot of years
Of good Psychology.
That's how I figured out
The problem wasn't he.

I didn't say how grand
Dinner out would be.
My friend has little money,
But he had still asked me…

All I felt was valid,
But he was not to blame.
I just didn't answer.
Avoiding it was lame.

Patricia A. Fisher

So, we had sorry feelings—
Instead of feeling fine,
So let me be assertive.
The problem was all mine.

Dear Mr. Henneman (C)

Dearest Mr. Henneman,
I'd like to telephone…
I'd really like to tell you,
While I am all alone.

'My' Dennis is so good and kind.
I know that he loves me.
I love him back with all my
                    heart.
I think, "How can this be?"

Did God decide to make this gift,
And send it here to me?
Did He wrap it up real nice,
With wondrous quality?

Tell me, Mr. Henneman.
I know that you are smart.
Is it like what I have felt?
Did he give me his heart?

Patricia A. Fisher

I Want to LIVE!

I am sure, dear counselor,
That I gave mine to him.
For us to stop our loving,
Would cause the world to end...

We've always been together.
That's what the young ones say.
We're sort of like a relic.
Thirty two years today.

Patricia A. Fisher

Dear Mr. Henneman (D)

Dearest Mr. Henneman,
Because of brother Bill,
We are having lots of fun!
He really is a pill!

He makes up all these phrases
To make me plagiarize.
Then he starts us laughing.
We tell him, "That's not wise."

Goofing 'round the campfire,
Goes on for quite a while.
So much of this merriment,
Just makes me want to smile...

The very first time in 30 years
Bill and I had words.
First time in an argument,
'Twas really for the birds!

Patricia A. Fisher

I told him off, 'cause I was mad
That he did not pitch in!
He yelled back, and said to me,
"Will you please stop bitchin'?"

I said, "This is my home.
You're not wanted here!"
Ten more minutes later,
We hugged each other near.

For all these years, we never
                    fought...
But this still makes some sense.
For we are closer than before.
We're no more on the fence.

Life went on. We felt ok.
Until that very next night.
I was trying to talk to him,
But he was a little 'tight'.

Patricia A. Fisher

I Want to LIVE!

He's talkative while drinking.
I can't be heard by him.
It is a bit nerve-wracking
What I felt was grim...

We love each other very much.
On this we do agree.
Once in awhile we'll hit a bump.
That's humanity!

Dearest Mr. Henneman,
This person I speak of,
Is such a pain, in the ass!
He's also full of love.

Patricia A. Fisher

Dear Mr. Henneman (E)

Dearest Mr. Henneman,
I hope you're feeling fine.
I would like to say to you
"The pleasure is all mine!"

To tell you 'bout
How good you are –
How you share
With the earth.

I'd like to say
You do good work.
Do you know
What that's worth?

Because of you,
Since we began,
I've gotten through
Bad times.

Patricia A. Fisher

They have been
Much shorter.
They're always
Up hill climbs.

I've come to know you
Just a bit.
Respecting
What I see…

Of how you
Help so many,
Just like
You've helped me.

You never want
A 'thank you'.
You fight this
Like the plague!

All you say is,
"It's my job!"
Your answer
Isn't vague…

I've heard that
Saying thank you,
To a
Human being,

Is not the way
It's 'spose to be.
It limits
Everything,

Because, in truth,
It's done by God.
We are but
A witness.

Patricia A. Fisher

When we say thanks
To ourselves,
We're bragging 'bout
Our fitness.

So, what I want
To say to you,
I don't know what
To share,

Because I want
To let you know
I'm very glad
You care.

Just one little person
Can help a million more.
I feel that you are doing this –
Like opening a door...

You give
One challenged person
A different
Point of view

To change
Their disposition,
And then
Support them too.

So, you have been
Appointed
To help
And understand

Many, many
Clients
By someone
Really grand!

Patricia A. Fisher

You are but
An instrument
Of love, respect
And truth.

For one thing,
I have never
Heard you
Be uncouth!

You have
A higher power.
(I'm guessing)...
Yet, I find,

You take your work
So seriously,
And you are
Very kind.

There is something
Serious
That you
Are going through.

Ever since
It happened,
Concern I have
For you...

I leave you
Little phone calls.
In hopes
To give support.

I am looking
Forward
To hear a
Good report,

Patricia A. Fisher

'Bout how you're
Feeling better,
And, Oh,
How clear your mind!

I would like
To give support.
For you are
In a bind!

You seem to
Have a crisis
Of your
Very own.

So, ask for help
From others.
Don't take this ride
Alone...

Pat

Chains

There have been chains on my heart for about a month. Tears come easy, and depression is prevalent. No matter what I do, I can't shake this feeling that I have to be extra good, or extra talented. I thought this would make it ok, with people, that I have a mental illness...

This way, maybe the stigma would dissipate, and Dennis and I would get that job at a nearby campground.

We would be very good at it, as we love camping! Maybe any problem with my illness would be more in balance, because Dennis and I would be together.

Patricia A. Fisher

This has all been so disturbing. My poor husband has been beside me all the way. He has listened to me, held me, and has covered me with blankets. He has probably wondered, like me, when this would pass - if ever...

I just spoke to someone, of good standing at the campground. They said they loved my writing. It was just what I needed to hear! It made me feel so good, but I don't know how long this feeling will last. For we have not yet been chosen for the job...

Joel says God works best, when a person talks as if something good is already in progress.

I Want to LIVE!

I am strong. I can do this. I can make it…

I use these tools, when my tremor is extra bad, and I notice a 25% improvement.

Yet, nothing's fair.

We all have our difficulties we must face. I guess, one of mine, is my being judged because of an illness I happen to have…

I have never hurt anyone in my 55 years. Yet stigma precedes me wherever I go…

Out of My Control

I have become aware of fellow mental health consumers on a more personal basis. Now that it's happened, I find that many of us have suicidal thoughts!

I want to share how I get away from these feelings, and go on with my life. I can go way down, then make it my business to come back up, without spending loads of time there...

The formula for this activity is probably different for every person, but I now can share how I no longer waste so much time feeling like I want to die.

It appears that, for a long time now, I do not want to waste time. Feeling bad, to me, is definitely a waste of precious time!

So, when I get to a place where I feel like I need to call someone for help, I call. I keep talking and listening until I get the kind of connection I need. Then, I grab onto that idea, or piece of information, and run with it!

My symptoms seem different each time I'm in trouble, so I need a different answer every time. The fear is very strong with every occurrence. It's as if it never happened to me before.

Just recently, about one year ago, I realized that I have the same stamina as just about anyone who I go to for psyche help. I have the same stamina as just about any person, as we are all swimming trying to keep our heads above water.

It was a wonderful realization! I feel more equal and I don't feel as if I have to lean so hard on fellow earthlings anymore…

You never know what they have gone through that day or the night before… They are only human, too (though I have my suspicions at times)…

Years ago, my niece helped me realize how tightly I was holding on to the world, trying to control other peoples' pain.

I love people, and maybe my higher power is telling me again, that I cannot control another person – even if they seem to be at death's door!

A wonderful therapist named Dee, told me that all I can do is support a person, (Help someone help themselves).
Dee, I never forgot...

Some of my new cohorts find it necessary to 'hug the ground' making themselves less of a target for other feelings. They appear to feel only depression.

When I have reached out to them, they have said "No" to any kind of fun or enjoyment.

I would like to tell my fellow mental health consumers that it's ok to feel a lot of feelings. They can still live good lives, and they will not perish from the change of one emotion to the other. They may even like having fun, or some other emotion besides depression.

I have been told that my suicidal thoughts happen to me more than they do to most people, but I also have been told that I don't stay down very long...

I've been told that I'm just well enough to be uncomfortable...

This is because I don't stay in any one emotion very long, yet I have visited all of them at one time or another.

I take chances that I will be rejected, unloved, hurt, ridiculed, abandoned, or just feel that all familiar, melancholy...

I usually find the good stuff in people. It's these times that make me keep reaching out on a regular basis – sometimes when I am in symptoms... (but it is more difficult then)!

I live knowing I will get suicidal. My suicidal ideations may have something to do with a temper tantrum I had as a child.

Maybe I did not get my way, or my needs met, and I remember screaming.

Now, when something doesn't go quite right for me, sometimes I get very angry and scared. Only now, as an adult, I want to end my life.

Other people I've met seem to put themselves into harmful situations. I've tried to control that, too. I've begged them to stop, and find a new way of life! They stay put, while speaking of their fear and discomfort…

I am afraid some one will die. They see the danger, and some may thrive on it!

A lot of us may need to be put on this danger list, because we physically don't take care of ourselves very well. We, too, see the danger and conveniently forget to take our medicine, eat the right foods, and exercise on a regular basis. We may drink too much and take illicit drugs.

Some of these are socially acceptable, and passed off as our being normal, and are even called human nature…

The people I spoke of earlier are such good human beings, and I love them. Yet, I can't tell them what to do – even to save their lives!

Maybe they want me to take better care of my physical ailments, too… I suppose I could die from this diabetes I have been fighting. I lack discipline sometimes, and make some choices that are not real healthy for me.

I think and feel that we humans are all unique – whether or not we live this uniqueness.

Sadly, *and* thankfully, I believe God is the only force that can control life and death, but I can still share what I use to help myself.

I can tell people how I put 25 Tools for Living in my seventh book, *From This Day Forward.*

Patricia A. Fisher

I Want To Live is my eighth book, and I keep sharing everything I've learned, in 35 years of therapy, by way of these books. Me, my husband, and our higher power, are all in support of my writing and publishing them. We have felt this since the beginning in 1996.

I pray often that they will reach the people who need them most.

I am now reminded, with this journaling, that there is very little I can control – even in myself.

More and more, I am leaving everything to my Heavenly Father. I am now, absolutely, not in control of anything another person feels, thinks, or does!

I do not rule the world! All I can do is 'guide my ship' as well as I can. I will no longer tell other people what to do! They don't do it anyway... That's it! No more! This is truly *Out of My Control!*

At least until tomorrow...

Patricia A. Fisher

Laugh at the Devil

Hell is a waste of time.
Periodically I hit bottom...

The devil lives here. The devil thrives on humans who lose their way.

At this moment, I am thankful. So, it is difficult for me to share how it is when evil consumes me.

My illness and evil walk hand in hand. They are bosom buddies. They are best friends. They are the same...

They feast on my well-being, as if it was their last meal. They team up to crush my every happy thought, and it gives them energy for my eventual slaughter.

But, I fool them! I have still been able to have a good life.

I crash occasionally. I still waste some time. I still lose my way. I am still tortured from time to time, and I am still burned in the fires of hell.

A million times I have broken the shell of my illness. There are so many better ways to live my life. Many times I must fight very hard to come back.

But, right now, I am at peace.

I find myself thanking God for the breeze on my arms and face, and for the exhilarating feeling that I have about His creations.

I smile from deep inside, and hell is nowhere around. The devil must be asleep, and my illness is letting me rest.

I find such joy just going for a walk, watching the clouds, or thinking about the people I love.

It is at these times, I am filled with gratitude, and it is at these times, I Laugh at the Devil...

Patricia A. Fisher

Buried Alive

That's where I was without choices...

At 55 years of age, I was told, in no uncertain terms, to give up many of my little treasures. These were things like coffee, cheese, carbonated beverages, and sugar.

Twelve years ago, I gave up alcohol. It's been thirty five years since I was a cigarette smoker...

I began to feel buried by all the musts and must-nots of my doctors.

I got so depressed that suicide was, again, on my list of possibilities.

I don't know how long I carried out the wishes of others, and felt as if the world was on my shoulders.

This afternoon, I found myself indulging in several must-nots. I had a very large, and very wonderful, candy bar. I ate foods without the slightest idea of how many carbohydrates they contained, and followed this with a size grande, Ethiopia Sidamo Coffee at Starbucks.

I was sitting at a small table, just outside the store, still somewhat depressed. I was hoping the great outdoors, and taboo caffeine, would shake something loose in my Psyche.

Just then, a woman got out of her mail van, and headed for the door of Starbucks.

She called to me and asked me if I was enjoying my coffee.

I responded with a firm, "Yes I am!"

She said, that this was going to be her "gotta have it cup"!

Those were magic words! I suddenly heard myself think the word, "choices".

Then I realized that there are going to be, "gotta have it" times in my own life.

I realized, finally, that I am the captain of my own ship, and the director of my own life.

I lost sight, along the way, of how we each must "choose our own poison."

I realized how much power I was relinquishing to others, by not choosing for myself.

Sitting there, with coffee in hand, I realized that making choices for myself is a lot more fun than entertaining suicide...

I Want to LIVE!

Thus, each choice I make in the future will be insurance that I will never again be 'buried alive'!

And, when my time does come, and I breathe my last breath, I hope to pass on with a smile on my face, knowing that I had lived, at least my golden years, on my own terms.

My Sisters, With Love

I wrote you a letter
        To put in my book.
It never felt right!
        What effort it took!

So, let this suffice –
        This writing of mine.
I tried not to grumble,
        And tried not to whine.

I'm only human.
        And don't want to fight!
When we're together,
        Flames just ignite!

I wrote to you –
        The truth that I see.
Sit down and read,
        And you might agree,

Patricia A. Fisher

'Bout how we've been hurt
    Yes it is true.
You have hurt me,
    And I have hurt you.

All that we want
    Is just love, of course.
We are who we are,
    Without any force.

We are not people,
    Told how to 'be'.
We all have choices.
    We want to be free.

Past indiscretions
    Get in the way
Of we three sisters.
    Hear what I say!

How can we show
      The love that we feel,
When each one of us
      Cannot be real?

All of those traits,
      That make me or you,
Cause us that anger.
      That just will not do!

All that I want –
      I hope you'll agree,
Is in the word love –
      Four letters you see...

My thoughts about peace
      Are written right here,
If only we sisters
      Could let go of fear...

Patricia A. Fisher

My Dennis

There's a story to be told here, and today, I'm going to tell it!

There's this little boy, who was born and raised in Ohio, USA. He was born in a hospital the 'usual' way – no test tubes or artificial anything like what we do these days…

His parents were considered middle class, and were well liked and respected.

They lived in what later became their garage. For the boy's Father was building their whole house a little at a time.

Part of the building materials came from some other building in town, and they were still very good quality, as the home still stands today – 54 years later...

The Mom in this family was fortunate to be a stay-at-home Mom, which she did very well. There were clean clothes in this little boy's closet and drawers. He woke up each morning with breakfast on the table, and came home to a healthy snack after school. Supper was at about the same time every evening.

His family went to church just about every Sunday. While they were gone, there would be a roast cooking in the oven for when they returned.

Once in awhile, they would pack up soda pop in a bucket of ice, and go to the neighborhood drive-in theatre. He and his two brothers watched what their parents chose for them. Later, when they were older, they walked to a theatre of their choice, and saw what they wanted to see.

When they were of school age, every year they would all go to the shoe store, and all the boys got a nice pair of school shoes. In the summer they would each get a pair of canvas shoes. They would not have the last word on the style and price, but they did get heard and a compromise would take place.

In short, this young man had a pretty great childhood. It had only one hang-up. He was not supposed to show any anger, which has caused him some difficulty through life. Yet, he is a far cry from being hurtful of himself or others.

One time, his parents chose not to tell him about a tonsillectomy he was to undergo. He did not know till he was in the hospital. Yet his father stayed with him all night long, and his mom stayed with him all day.

There is more to tell… The young man in question became a boy scout, which fits nicely into his 'Leave it to Beaver' upbringing. Later, he got a job after school, mostly selling suits at Sears.

Again, he was well liked and respected, and was allowed some freedoms that others were not.

Next was Ohio State University, beginning September of 1966. He was a student there for 2 years. Of all things, he shares that he had a poor scholastic average! So, he left college to join the Air Force, where he served proudly for almost 4 years.

The service took him to Denver, to San Antonio, Texas, and then Florida, Thailand and the Philippines. He had no culture shock that I know of, and has shared his wonderful experiences with many people.

Patricia A. Fisher

He became interested in electricity, and worked as a Weapons Control Systems Technician. He worked on acquisition and guidance radar systems.

After the service, he traveled back to Colorado, where he got a job, and met the girl next door – *me*...

We started dating, and soon he purposed marriage. I said "No". After awhile I purposed to him. He said, "Yes". We were married 6 weeks later.

Dennis Howard Fisher and Patricia Anne Holley were married November 17, 1973.

We met 32 years ago, and have been married over 30 of those years.

Dennis is a person I have loved and respected for a very long time. He lights up my life on a daily basis, by just doing 'Dennis' stuff. He is just human, but he is a really good human. He is very, very smart, and I think his professors didn't see him in the right light...

He worked in communications as a Cable Engineer. He worked day in and day out. He probably missed work less than 2 weeks in his 27 years of service. He was offered a promotion at retirement, and said, "No" with a smile on his face. (We had plans to travel in our new RV!)

I am writing this story, about my good husband, right here in that RV, and I can't be more satisfied with how we are spending our retirement. Dennis and I are together more than ever, and he is sitting about 3 feet away from me, as I write his story...

We are staying in a campground in the Rocky Mountains. This is what retirement is all about! Dennis feels very fortunate, even with how very hard he worked all those years. My favorite part of retirement is being with 'my' Dennis. His is being with me in a peaceful environment like this...

The following stories are about some of my favorite places to visit – and the surrounding areas.

They speak of differences between prairie, desert, and mountainous areas, and how they are all beautiful in the eyes of many travelers.

𝒫𝒶𝓉𝓇𝒾𝒸𝒾𝒶 𝒜. ℱ𝒾𝓈𝒽𝑒𝓇

Been There

Have you ever been in a race with a turtle and lost? Sound impossible? Remember the story about "The Tortoise and the Hare?" It was a lot like that...

We were staying at a campground called, **"Berry Bend Campground" in Missouri.** We met some good people there, Donna, Dave, and Bill. One of whom *has to have* the same camping space we *have to have*!

This is the place where the black birds almost carry you off! This is the place I raced with a rather large turtle...

Patricia A. Fisher

We were driving along one of the country roads in the area, when I noticed a good size turtle. I saw another and another. We found out that this area harbored maybe hundreds of these animals.

I was sort of goofy that day anyway, and when I saw this turtle, I stopped the car on the side of the road. This turtle was already on its way across, so I joined it running in slow motion.

Actually, there really wasn't a winner that day. I have to confess… I chickened out half way across, because the turtle was so fast!

By the way, how many of you can say you had a race with a turtle? It's simply not done on a regular basis!

It turns out, that when we were about to leave, one of the turtles came to our space to see us off. It was very thoughtful, as our new, little friend probably knew of the race between its cousin and me.

I was informed by the 'Turtle Racing Committee' that, because I quit the race half way across the road, my racing buddy won the race by default.

There you have it! That's my story and I'm sticking to it!

_____

One other trip, about 20 miles east of **New Orleans, Louisiana,** we drove into a campground at St. Bernard State Park, and saw an armadillo – of all things! We found that they were roaming around all over the place!

Later, we took a walk and at the other end of the campground, we heard the deafening sound of what must have been bionic frogs! We decided that if we were staying on that side of the park, we would never get any sleep...

Since it was night time, we carried a flashlight in the dark.

All of a sudden, the bushes rustled about 50 feet away. I could just picture this giant frog stocking us! I grabbed Dennis' hand and pulled him back to our RV, as he laughed and laughed.

This all happened,
'Down in Louisiana'...

When we went to the **State of Washington,** we were overwhelmed by the flowers. All along the streets there were hanging baskets, so full of flowers that just seemed to call to us, "Look at us!"

Other places outside Washington, you can see just flowers, but up around the state of Washington, they are vibrant with color! They're huge and healthy, and just begging you to look!

_____

At **Port Angeles, Washington** we enjoyed a pier, where a seal was bobbing up and down, looking at all of us more than we were looking at it!

At this port you can take a ferry to **Victoria, British Colombia,** just across the water into Canada. There you will find a beautiful place called, "Bouchard Gardens". People everywhere have told us of this place.

They all say the same thing about it, "Go there!"

From what I understand, there is what is called 'A High Tea'... This sounds like so much fun! We plan to go the first chance we get...

Have you ever been on the **Gulf Coast of Mississippi?** This is definitely a 'must see'. I didn't even know Mississippi was on the Gulf Coast!

Of course, the water is warm, and the waves are very low. Highway 90 runs along the well-kept beach of white sand on one side, and those huge, pristine houses on the other.

These houses are just like the old plantation houses, with the big pillars on the front porches. The main difference is how much land these coastal houses have around them.

Along this drive, you will find a restaurant called Chappy's.

It is an excellent place to eat, and specializes in blackened Red Fish. They serve 3 or 4 flavors of butter – one flavor being from real alligator. There are actually real, un-messed-with, pieces of alligator in there! (I wouldn't recommend it)…

The owner, Chappy, was still the big honcho when we were there 3 or 4 years ago. He's a friendly 'chap'!

I Want to LIVE!

This story would not be complete without the little, sneaky, invisible, tyrannical, ghastly, unstoppable, unsociable, disagreeable, NO-SEE-UMS!

You go to this place knowing, ahead of time, that the little beasts are ready and waiting for delicious tourists!

There are stupendous casinos lining the beach. If you'd like to gamble or see a live show, you will be impressed at the choices you'll have.

All told, you will be entertained, and the scenery itself is spell-binding!

———

Patricia A. Fisher

We've been so many beautiful places! Both the **Atlantic and the Pacific Oceans** have an atmosphere beyond anything or anywhere, except the Rocky Mountains.

───────────

25 years ago, we took a cruise to the **Virgin Islands.** The water there was so clear you could see about 20 feet down to the coral below. There were fish of many different colors, and some with stripes, swimming just under our bellies.

Dennis could not swim at the time, but the ocean was so salty, he floated as we snorkeled in that incredible water.

───────────

I Want to LIVE!

Puerto Rico, Haiti, St. Thomas, and St. John were on our particular tour.
Our ship was called, "The Italia". I have always been smitten by dark hair and brown eyes, so a ship full of Italian workers was just peachy with me!

The waiters on the Italia almost chopped off your arm, if you started to help yourself to the coffee or anything! That was their job and their livelihood, and they did not want to lose it!

We sat with a couple every dinner time. The man's name was Taylor. He and I would make certain sounds to describe the taste of the evenings wine. We had such fun!

On this cruise, I ate several foods that I would not even look at on dry land!

There were the frog legs, escargot (snails), Lobster Newburg and more...

When we would go ashore, we were so used to allowing for the rocking of the ship, we would walk a little zigzagged. One time, at one of the ports, we were waiting in line for burgers. Every so often, one of us would go, "whoa"! Balance was sometimes difficult just off the ship.

The Italia showed us a very good time, and didn't miss a thing.

Our night clothes were even placed on the bed in a certain way, and there was always fresh fruit in a basket every night. The staff was 'invisible'. We never saw the person in charge of our cabin…

There was always something fun to do, or you could just not do a thing! Gambling was also available. Live shows and the Captain's Ball were always good for dress-up. 6 meals a day took care of any pangs of hunger, and there were dances every night.

Looking over the side, you could see sun tanned young people diving for any coins that were dropped into the water.

On land, we saw and visited, with little Haitian children. Their clothing was limited, and some were half naked. The ladies in the back of our vehicle had been talking to these children.

These kids lived in thatch roofed huts with dirt floors. When they were swept, the floors were less dusty, but they were still dirt...

Meanwhile, I was noticing fruit trees in the area. I was glad they had at least something to fill their tummies.

I was really getting into how foreign everything was, and how the ladies were bridging the language barrier.

Then it was time to go. I heard one of the ladies call out, "Goodbye Joseph!" I had to smile...

It was like another world to me, and an adventure we will never forget!

We have walked dozens of beaches just around the **USA.** We are drawn to them, yet, we fear them, especially while sleeping near them at night.

San Simeon, in California, was one of these times. Our hotel was so close to the beach, we slept fitfully, thinking about the possibility of waves washing up the outer walls of our hotel.

Patricia A. Fisher

Somewhere along the **California Coast, between Monterey and San Francisco,** we came to a genuine, authentic, true blue, A&W Restaurant. It was right on the beach, and the waves were high.

We proceeded to drink our icy-cold, A&W root beer – out of frosty, root beer mugs. MMMMMMMMM...

I doubt if it is still there, but I would like to go back sometime...

These are some of the beaches I have not mentioned in this book. They were all beautiful, and candy to our eyes...

Hunting Island, SC
(Where we were first introduced to the dreaded NO-SEE-UMS...)

Plymouth Rock, MA
(Where pilgrims first stepped off the Mayflower. Next to the rock is a full size replica of the original Mayflower. The replica took the same journey. Also whale watching in this area)

Virginia Beach, VA

Myrtle Beach, SC

St Augustine Beach, FL

Clearwater Beach, FL

Patricia A. Fisher

**Cape Flattery, WA
(Most Northwestern point of the continental USA)**

**Cape Cod, MA
(More whale watching, and beautiful homes with no water or electricity-by ordinance)**

**Newport Beach, OR
(Home of MO'S restaurant where you can get a bucket of great New England, Clam Chowder)!**

As you wander down those coastal highways, you become intoxicated and get the idea you want to move to a beach. You price the real estate, and look around. You begin to think,

"This vacation is enough," and you begin to rationalize, "We can always come back next year…" You travel to the mountains. You start thinking about moving there. You think, "I want a cabin in the mountains." You discuss it with your significant other, and he or she is not as fond of this idea as you are. "Lets get a place near the city, and we can go to the theatre, etc." You end up staying where you are, and talk about your next two-week vacation.

This scenario goes on and on, each year, until you meet some people with an RV…

Never ask an RV owner about their RV, unless you have several hours to cuss and discuss!

They just won't stop talking about all the ins and outs of the RV world, and how they get around a particular challenge. They'll tell you where to get the lowest prices for insurance, where they've been, and where they are going. They'll tell you about how their ovens bake bread, and how they liked where they went last.

Well, we bought an RV! We realized that we could have that beachfront property, that cabin in the mountains, and a place on the desert. We can move away or stay put whenever we please. We RV people wave at each other coming in and going out. There is a friendly connection among us, and it is infectious…

Winding River
Winding River Campground, Grand Lake, Colorado

This wondrous place
Is a fantasy land
Beyond
My own belief!

There isn't
Any place like it!
I really
Don't want to leave!

Patricia A. Fisher

A herd of horses
Are brought about
For anyone
To ride.

They stand there
At the stable –
Their beauty
Not denied.

Then, at night,
They're herded back
To where they all
Belong.

Here is where
They eat and sleep.
'Bout them
I write this song.

A little pen
Containing goats
And chickens,
Ducks and pigs.

Right there
On that good land,
Where people
Park there rigs.

A little child,
With smiles galore,
Rides by
Upon a horse.

This is a memory
He will have.
He will come back,
Of course!

Patricia A. Fisher

Larger groups
Of equestrians
Mount up
To take a ride.

Off they go,
All at once,
Throughout
The countryside.

Lovely cabins
That people rent
Are here and there
Around.

Elk and other
Animals
Are free
To roam the ground.

A great big man –
His name is Wes.
He owns a lot
Or part,

Of this
Magnificent area,
That's so close
To our heart.

I do not know him
Personally,
But when he entered
The place,

I saw a man
Of power,
With goodness
On his face.

Patricia A. Fisher

It takes this kind
Of person
To work and run
This land.

Where people
Can pitch a tent,
Or camp
In rigs more grand.

I believe
There is a ranch
Not too
Far away.

It's also
"Winding River"
I saw it
Yesterday.

This whole place
Is beautiful!
It's shared
With open hand.

So that
Everybody
May know
And understand,

That there's
No other place like this –
So beautiful
And unique!

I hope that all
The rest of you
Will come
And take a peek.

Patricia A. Fisher

In a tree,
Where we are parked,
A woodpecker
Made its home.

It pecked a hole
Into a tree,
Where baby birds
Have grown.

Ice cream socials
During the week –
Just adding
To the fun,

So we can
Get together
Where one
Meets everyone!

I Want to LIVE!

Chuck wagon breakfasts
Or dinners,
Or, maybe,
A hayride,

Will keep you
Happily busy,
And feeling good
Inside!

I guess I've told you
Most of it –
Of how
I love this place.

Dear God,
Keep it going.
It brings smiles
To our face...

Patricia A. Fisher

Moab or Bust
Arches National Park, Utah

Dennis and I were headed for the Grand Canyon, by way of Moab, Utah. It was April of 1984.

It was very late. I suppose it was around midnight. We must have driven straight through from Denver on I-70 West.

Dennis and I were calmly riding along at about 60 mph. There was no moon, and the stars were behind the clouds. It was very dark with no lights anywhere… Not a house, or other building, could be seen, and very seldom a car would go by.

Just then, we saw a young man coming toward us on the right side of our car. He was riding a skateboard, as if it was common to be doing this, on an interstate highway, in the middle of a cold, dark night.

We looked at each other, and we asked, "Did you see what I saw?"

Neither of us could think of what to do next, so we just drove on, shaking our heads in disbelief, and chuckling a bit.

The only way we could see him, was with the headlights on the car. As soon as we passed, he could no longer be seen.

(We went back much later in the daylight, and still no houses or cars on the side of the road).

Later, we decided to take a shortcut to Moab. We turned onto Utah Highway 126.

We drove about 15 miles with no traffic, no houses, no lights, and no moon or stars. We came across a tiny town with a small gas station that was closed. The three buildings we saw around there also had no lights on. Nobody lived in this quaint little place.

This is when we saw a narrow bridge, painted white. We judged it to be only 8 feet wide, and 100 yards long.

Patricia A. Fisher

It stretched clear across the Colorado River, and there was no way we could turn around...

Having no idea if it was strong enough to bare the weight of our car and small, hard-walled trailer, we started across.

There were only 6 inch clearances on each side of our car mirrors. The crossing was slow...

You must realize. It was the middle of the night!

We made it across!

Then came the desert wash. This is like a river or stream bed – sometimes containing water – sometimes not.

I Want to LIVE!

This night it had water in it. Guess who volunteered to wade out into the water to see how deep it was. 'Dummy me' took off my shoes, and walked out in front of our car into the wash. It turned out to be only one foot deep.

As I look back on this memory, I understand why some folks find it easy to call me just a little bit crazy. (smile)

Twenty miles after the wash, we began to see camper's lights along the Colorado. They were dim, but none the less, they were lights!

Finally, we were in Moab, where we stayed the rest of the morning.

Patricia A. Fisher

Arches National Park had a natural structure made out of red rock. It was very popular with people wanting to photograph the area.

We were standing about 200 yards from the arch, where there were two people with cameras.

Dennis and I were talking quietly. We asked each other, "When on earth are they going to leave so we can have our turn?"

After they left, Dennis went over to the arch.

We discovered that the other couple heard everything we said, because even quiet conversation could easily be heard – even at 200 yards.

We had a laugh, because the other couple had pretended not to hear us at all.

It is a fun memory for us, and all of it happened in the first two days of that vacation!

Patricia A. Fisher

Sages and Grey
Brantley Lake State Park, New Mexico

I think I hear the sizzle
Of rain upon the sand.

The fragrance is delicious
(Of sunshine baking land).

I think I heard a thank you
In a quiet desert voice.

Speaking in a whisper,
Inhabitants rejoice,

"Thank you for the moisture,
And rain upon our sand.

Our carpeting of sage and grey
Lays close against our land.

Patricia A. Fisher

Desert life begins to dance,
When winds begin to blow.

How reverent we huddle close—
Is nature friend or foe?

Take cover little creatures
Of every shape and size.

We value every one of you.
You're candy to our eyes.

The storm is nearly over.
We no longer need to hide.

The desert winds have spoken.
Its inhabitants have cried,

I Want to LIVE!

Patricia A. Fisher

"Thank you, Mother Nature.
It all has been great fun!

The rain has fed our homeland.
Look! Here comes the sun!"

All is back to normal.
The days are bright and clear.

Lazy from the sunshine,
I watch this land so dear.

The wide and open spaces
Beckon me to come.

Without the words of humans,
It sounds more like a hum.

I Want to LIVE!

If you don't look closely,
For a little while,

You will miss its beauty,
Mile after mile.

As a child, you'll wander.
As a child, you'll see.

Like candy all around you,
And ten years old you'll be...

Patricia A. Fisher

Out On the Prairie
(Jackson Lake State Park, Colorado)

I hear a pitter-patter
Of rain upon the roof.

The hour's very late,
And reminds me of my youth...

A storm would fall upon us.
I'd hide right by the door.

As rain came down in torrents,
The sun kept shining 'ore.

'Twas always quite exciting!
I'd love to smell the rain,

With lightening all around me,
And thunder's loud refrain.

Patricia A. Fisher

So, out here on the prairie,
With rain upon my roof,

I'm back there in my childhood.
It's thrilling! That's the truth!

Each drop of rain
Is valuable--

More valuable
Than gold.

For each small
Drop of water

Makes a difference
I am told.

Out here on the prairie
You see another life

Between the Rocky Mountains,
And the drier desert life.

I'm finding out
Some answers

To questions
That I have.

What are the gifts
Of prairie life?

(The skunks
Sure make me laugh!)

Patricia A. Fisher

Huge pelicans
Fly by your door!

You'll gasp
As you look on!

You'll find yourself
In disbelief!

They land
And then they're gone!

Beautiful pheasants,
Wild turkeys,

And songs of
Meadowlarks,

Rabbits, deer,
And killdeer birds,

Coyotes
And their 'barks'.

I feel bewildered,
And try to describe,

The greatness
Of this land!

Once it turns
The key to your heart

You will
Understand...

Patricia A. Fisher

Colors and shades
Of every hue—

Long shadows
On toward night,

Will call to you
In a different way.

You won't believe
The sight!

Entire rainbows
You can touch—

Both ends of them
In view,

I Want to LIVE!

Patricia A. Fisher

Instead of finding
Pots of gold,

There's something else
For you.

A work of art—
Incredible!

Both ends
That you can see,

Are right there
In the water.

Hypnotized
You'll be...

Tall grasses boast
Of yellows and orange,

And greens
You've never seen.

Burnt sienna
Everywhere!

The air is fresh
And clean!

Fragrances
Of blossoms

Will stop you
On your walk,

Patricia A. Fisher

And you'll be
Breathing deeper--

No need for you
To talk.

For words
Do not explain

What you'll
Feel inside.

We poets
Fail real often—

Even though
We've tried...

Farms with animals,
Far and wide,

Sheep, and cows,
And all.

Watching some of the
Little ones,

Can really
Be a ball!

Fields of wheat,
And corn, and hay,

Yes, there are
Pumpkins, too.

Patricia A. Fisher

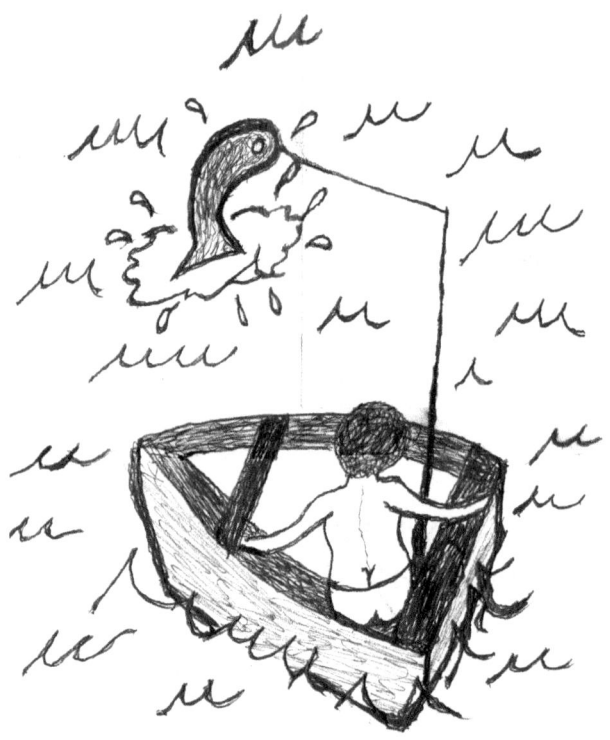

It can be
Like a holiday—

And I'm
Inviting you!

Big fish
Jump out of the water,

Tempting you
To try,

To catch
A couple for dinner.

They're better
Than fish you buy!

Patricia A. Fisher

You'll launch your boat
In the water,

If you are
So inclined.

You'll drift away
Out yonder,

And this might
Ease your mind.

Or you may like
Other water games—

Either on, or over,
The lake.

There is something
For every one.

It's here
For you to take.

That very self-same
Water

Is destination
Bound.

For down the line,
Our farmers,

Irrigate
Their ground.

Patricia A. Fisher

I've learned
About the prairie,

By looking
Past my nose,

At all the fabulous
Beauty,

Forgetting 'bout
My woes.

I'd like for you
To enjoy,

Every wonderful
Thing,

Out here on the
Prairie,

In the midst
Of spring…

Patricia A. Fisher

I Want to LIVE!

Patricia A. Fisher

Colorado, I'm Home

I'm home... I'm glad to be home.
My heart rises up, as I stop and stare. The mountains of jagged, mossy, cliffs, are phenomenal and beyond me.

I gasp for air at two miles high, because the air is thin, and because the pines are so majestic!

While listening to whispers, way up in those trees, the winds begin to blow harder. All the sounds of the forest play a symphony, as lovely as any angel's voice.

My heart remembers coming here as a child. Adventures were many...

Speaking of adventures and angels, we met a couple of angels while camping at a place just outside Rocky Mountain National Park. Low and behold, they had just purchased a motor home! It was the same make and model as ours, so we immediately had some things in common we could talk about!

It was more than RVs-in-common that drew Cindy and Steve closer to us. This couple spoke of many familiar things -- including their wish to travel.

They'd like to travel with only a few people.

They have recently retired at 50 years of age…

Cindy likes to make bread, like me. She shared one of her secrets for good bread, and spoke of a pan of brownies she made in her RV oven. She loves to cook, like me also.

They love to camp and travel! (They just don't know it yet)! All they've had so far is 2 short weeks of vacation in their new RV, and they have had only a bit of the excitement that their future holds! (They don't know that either)!

Cindy and Steve are catching the RV bug, and we can't be happier for them!

It's time to play, you guys… Maybe you'll remember what we said, "Retirement is when you know you have found your calling…"

Colorado is still beautiful, and it is home… Yet, there are many places we've been, in this country, that are beautiful in their own right.

See you on the road, you guys! We're looking forward to it!

Patricia A. Fisher